SELF-REGULATED LEARNING FOR ACADEMIC SUCCESS

How do I help students manage their thoughts, behaviors, and emotions?

Carrie
GERMEROTH | Crystal
DAY-HESS

ASCD   Alexandria, VA USA

Website: www.ascd.org   www.ascdarias.org
E-mail: books@ascd.org

Printed in the United States of America. Cover art © 2013 by ASCD. ASCD publications present a variety of viewpoints. The views expressed or implied in this book should not be interpreted as official positions of the Association.

ASCD LEARN TEACH LEAD® and ASCD ARIAS™ are trademarks owned by ASCD and may not be used without permission. All other referenced trademarks are the property of their respective owners.

PAPERBACK ISBN: 978-1-4166-1856-0   ASCD product #SF114041

Also available as an e-book (see Books in Print for the ISBNs).

Library of Congress Cataloging-in-Publication Data
Germeroth, Carrie.
  Self-regulated learning for academic success : how do I help students manage their thoughts, behaviors, and emotions? / Carrie Germeroth and Crystal Day-Hess.
     pages cm
  Includes bibliographical references.
  ISBN 978-1-4166-1856-0 (pbk. : alk. paper) 1. Self-culture. 2. Learning. 3. Motivation in education. 4. Academic achievement. I. Title.
  LC32.G49 2013
  371.39'43—dc23
                              2013036762

21 20 19 18 17 16 15 14 13   1 2 3 4 5 6 7 8 9 10

SELF-REGULATED LEARNING FOR ACADEMIC SUCCESS

How do I help students manage their thoughts, behaviors, and emotions?

Want to earn a free ASCD Arias e-book?
Your opinion counts! Please take 2–3 minutes to give
us your feedback on this publication. All survey
respondents will be entered into a drawing to
win an ASCD Arias e-book.

Click here or type in this web location:
www.ascd.org/ariasfeedback

Thank you!

The What, Why, and How of Self-Regulation

As every teacher knows, student learning is influenced by a complex set of factors, and there's no single formula that can ensure success. But as a teacher, you also know you have a powerful role to play. An essential way to help students develop the critical thinking and independent learning skills they need to succeed academically is by supporting self-regulation in the classroom.

What is self-regulation? Simply defined, it is the ability to control one's body and self, to manage one's emotions, and to maintain focus and attention (Shonkoff & Phillips, 2000). Self-regulation begins to develop in early childhood, and, according to the model first articulated by developmental psychologist Lev Vygotsky (1997), it proceeds in stages:

- *Stage 1:* Children are regulated by another person, typically a parent or a teacher. This outside regulator provides the rules for behavior and monitors the children while they learn how to apply these rules to themselves.
- *Stage 2:* Children begin to internalize rules for behavior and conduct and to apply these rules to other people. Although it's typical for teachers and parents to discourage tattling, when young children tell on one another or point out that others are "doing

things wrong," it's a positive sign that they're starting to notice both rules and rule violations.

- *Stage 3:* Children begin to apply the rules of behavior and conduct to themselves, and they do so voluntarily even when no one is watching them. It's at this point that children may be able to stop themselves from doing something "against the rules" and initiate actions that follow the rules.

Self-Regulation in the Classroom

Within the context of education, self-regulation can be thought of as the fourth "R"; it's an ability students need not only to set and achieve academic goals in reading, writing, and arithmetic but also to interact appropriately with others in the classroom. The foundational nature of self-regulation explains why it is so often linked with the general concept of school readiness. Indeed, the following skills, identified in a national survey of kindergarten teachers as critical to school readiness, are all closely tied to self-regulation:

- Communicating needs, wants, and thoughts verbally
- Sustaining attention and being enthusiastic and curious in new activities
- Inhibiting impulsivity and following directions
- Taking turns and being sensitive to other children's feelings (Blair, 2003, p. 1)

We know that students' physical and social environments can have a profound effect on how well they do in school, and plenty of evidence suggests the same is true of students' ability to self-regulate. The self-regulation skills of preschoolers have actually been linked to their eventual SAT scores. Difficulty with self-regulation translates into poor work habits, trouble concentrating, low motivation, and behavioral problems, some so extreme that they lead to expulsion.

The good news is that self-regulation in the classroom is something that can be modeled and taught—not just in the "ideal window" of early childhood but throughout a student's schooling (Boekaerts, 2006). Students' ability to manage their "thoughts, behaviors, and emotions in order to successfully navigate their learning experiences" is known as *self-regulated learning* (Zumbrunn, Tadlock, & Roberts, 2011, p. 4).

The Phases of Self-Regulated Learning

Like Zimmerman (2008), we recommend looking at self-regulated learning as a three-phase process.

During the pre-learning **forethought phase**, students focus on the expectations of a new task, what they expect the upcoming task's outcomes to be, and the interest in or value they place on the task. In other words, students consider how much they care about what they're about to do and how well they believe they can do it. It's during the forethought phase that students set goals for themselves and plan how they will approach the challenge or solve the problem. Where will they begin? What strategies will they use? How much are they willing to do?

During the **performance phase** that follows, students apply their chosen strategy to do the actual "what" of the work. This is the time for internal troubleshooting. Students consider what is or is not working and what is or is not engaging or rewarding. Critically, they also decide whether they need help or guidance, whether they will stick to a task or abandon it, and what adjustments they need to make to complete the work.

Finally, during the **self-reflection phase**, students respond to and reflect on the task and its outcomes. How much effort did they invest? What worked and what didn't? What approach might be a better choice next time? Ideally, students will apply these self-judgments to future learning, which will then effect the *next* forethought phase.

Zimmerman's three-phase model underscores that with practice and the right teacher support all students can become successful self-regulated learners. By drawing on their previous learning experiences, they can assemble a better toolkit of strategies and build confidence in their ability to take on new challenges. By contrast, if students don't believe that they can learn, they may not even attempt challenging tasks. And if they don't reflect on the work that they do, the strategies they use, and the outcomes they achieve, they are less likely to use effective learning strategies in the future (Schunk & Ertmer, 2000).

Teachers can help students manage their thoughts, behaviors, and emotions in the classroom by modeling appropriate strategies and creating supportive yet academically challenging learning environments. In this publication, we present research-based instructional strategies keyed to preK and kindergarten, elementary school, and middle and high school that you can implement today to support your students throughout each phase of self-regulated learning.

Developing self-regulation is an iterative process, and the strategies we present are designed to help students build and extend their skills as they move through school. Don't be afraid to try strategies associated with grade levels lower than the level you teach. If, for example, you have an 8th grader who struggles to follow rules and stay on task, the scaffolding supports we recommend for elementary-age students are likely to be very helpful. Of course, many of our suggested strategies—such as modeling a positive attitude toward learning and providing simple mediation strategies— are appropriate for all grade levels and every classroom.

Self-Regulated Learning in PreK and Kindergarten

Young children just beginning to gain regulatory control over their attention, actions, and emotions learn best in environments that are playful. If you're a preK or kindergarten teacher, a general way to help your students develop self-regulation is by emphasizing make-believe play—guiding them to create imaginary situations in which they act out specific roles. The broad content themes of early childhood curricula can be adapted fairly easily to provide more intentional opportunities for this kind of play. For example, during a "Wind and Water" theme, students might play pretend "hurricane" in one classroom, "aquarium" in another, and "underwater explorers" in yet another, each time following the rules of their "characters" and the scenario.

Let's take a closer look at how to support self-regulation in the youngest students during each phase of Zimmerman's three phases of self-regulation.

Supporting Forethought (PreK–K)

Remember, forethought occurs before learning activities and is largely about motivation, interest, and the confidence to take on the task. Because young students are naturally curious about their environment and engaged in learning, supporting forethought in preK and kindergarten is about encouraging these positive thoughts and behaviors. At this age, a teacher- and child-led instructional approach is optimal. By this, we mean that the students have some freedom to "design" activities, based on their own interest, and the teacher follows that direction, providing background information to enrich play and learning scenarios and thoughtfully creating new learning opportunities based on the how the play evolves.

What to Do: Plan for Play

Planning for imaginative play supports self-regulation because you're asking the students to think ahead about what they're going to play and then setting the expectation that they will follow through with that plan; in this way, it prefigures the planning older students will do to achieve learning goals. When you brainstorm play scenarios with young students, you increase their engagement in the activity to come and improve your ability to authentically assess their understanding of a topic or concept.

Ideas to Try Now

☐ **Turn topics students are interested in into complex play themes.** For example, they may keep coming back to the topic of pets (their own pets or pets they'd like to have), or you may notice several students pretending to be cats or dogs—or lions or bears! Think of a way to turn that interest into a more complex play theme that can support multiple roles and scenarios. An interest in animals, for example, lends itself to a veterinarian or zoo play theme.

☐ **Use a story, video, field trip, or guest speaker to stimulate interest and build background knowledge.** For our pet example, you might invite a local veterinarian to visit your classroom and talk about what the job is like day to day.

Supporting Performance (PreK–K)

When it comes to completing a task, preschoolers and kindergartners may need scaffolding. One of the central concepts of Vygotskian theory is the idea of *mental tools*—things like shopping lists and mnemonic devices that help people focus, remember, understand, imagine, and calculate.

What to Do: Use Simple Visual Tools to Support Memory

An *external mediator*—a tangible, outside object like a picture or a string around a finger—is one of the first mental tools young children can master (Bodrova & Leong, 2007). When children count on their fingers, they're using an external mediator that gradually instills the mental process of counting; once they internalize the process, they don't need the tool any more. Just as visual tools, such as manipulatives, help young children master mathematics content, using tangible and visual reminders supports early self-regulation during all kinds of learning activities.

Ideas to Try Now

☐ **Give learners who have trouble remembering to put their names on their papers a pair of glasses with the lenses removed.** Call them their "editor's eyes" and ask them to use them to remind themselves to check their work before turning it in (Bodrova & Leong, 2008).

☐ **Pair students for reading activities and give them photos or drawing of a set of lips and a pair of ears mounted on separate pieces of paper.** The child whose turn it is to read holds the lips, while the listener holds the ears; then they switch. This visual reminder of their roles helps them maintain attention during the task (Bodrova et al., 2012).

What to Do: Model a Positive Attitude Toward Learning

A positive mindset is especially important during challenging activities, when students must choose between "It's too hard; I can't" and "It's hard, but I'll try." You want to demonstrate the process of talking through a problem so that your students will begin to see how to negotiate challenging situations. This is an instructional strategy that is applicable at every grade level.

Ideas to Try Now

☐ **Introduce the process of observing, researching, creating and testing hypotheses, and collaborating to find answers or new ways to solve problems.** Explain to your students that together, you're going to identify a problem through observation, research possible solutions, and try to find the answers to your problem. Create visual records of your quest, using pictures when possible, to make sure preliterate learners can follow along.

☐ **Help students realize that answers don't always come easily. Persistence is a key facet of self-regulation.** By regularly modeling this "I'll try and keep trying" attitude when confronting challenges in the classroom, you are giving your students a template for how to tackle tasks in later grades and in life.

What to Do: Provide Simple Mediation Strategies

Although we often exhort children to "use their words" or "work it out" during a disagreement, we don't always provide them with explicit strategies for how to do so. But just as children need to be taught the fundamentals of literacy or math, they also need the building blocks of conflict resolution. Begin with tangible, hands-on methods. The goal is to illustrate ways to resolve conflict other than fighting or arguing. This is an instructional strategy that is applicable at every grade level.

Ideas to Try Now

☐ **Settle preK disputes using a "dispute bag."** PreK students tend to argue most about issues like who gets to use or play with a certain object or sit in a favorite space. In these scenarios, put a set of playing cards in a bag and allow each child to pick a card. Then, in order, starting with whoever has the highest (or lowest) card, each child picks a book, puzzle, a place to sit, or whatever the objective in dispute may be.

☐ **Settle preK and kindergarten disputes using language.** Have children write or draw plans for what they will play with or do during center time. You can structure the center time so that children can't all choose to do the same thing. When children argue over who gets to use various materials for play or games, have them reference their plans to solve the dispute. You'll find that when children learn that print carries a message and their plan for play means something, you won't need to step in to manage the conflict—they'll resolve it themselves.

Supporting Self-Reflection (PreK–K)

The self-reflection phase looks a little different in the lower grades than it does in the higher ones, because children this age can struggle to tell the difference between what's real and what they want to be real. Although some studies suggest that young children can engage in self-evaluation and may be able to judge their own competence fairly (Anderson & Adams, 1985), other research casts doubt on their ability to provide a true estimate of their skills (Wilson & Trainin, 2007).

With their self-concepts just beginning to form, young children tend to look to the perceptions of grownups to inform their own sense of competence. This means they are especially susceptible to parent and teacher evaluations and feedback.

What to Do: Give the Right Kind of Praise and Feedback

Praise is a mixed bag. Although it can increase students' self-efficacy and their expectations of future success, it can also lead them to feel helpless in the face of challenges if their self-worth is tied too closely to being praised. In other words, when we praise students by saying "You did so well on that assignment! You must be really smart!" we set them up to feel "stupid" any time they don't do well—or to avoid challenge for fear that failure will mean they're no longer "smart." Linking performance to intelligence also tends to focus students more on task outcomes (the grade or score they get) than on the learning associated with the task.

By contrast, praise for effort ("Wow, you worked really hard at solving that problem!") focuses students on the benefits of hard work. When a child learns to associate task outcomes with the effort invested, he's more likely to attribute failure to a lack of effort and to adopt new strategies and work harder until he succeeds. Again, this strategy is recommended for all grade levels.

Ideas to Try Now

☐ **Provide praise that is sincere.** Your praise should include specific information about what the student did well, and it should be provided only when warranted.

☐ **Attribute performance to factors within the students' control.** When students succeed, be sure to call out something they did to achieve the positive outcome—their effort, for example, or the strategies they used. Avoid linking success to intelligence or luck.

☐ **Promote autonomy.** Make sure your students have the tools necessary to do each task and assure them you will help them learn what they need to complete the task on their own. This isn't about favoring independent work over group work; it's about reinforcing students' confidence that they are able to do what's required.

☐ **Eliminate activities or practices that compare students with one another.** Not only can comparisons lower the self-esteem of anyone who is not a "top" student, they can create a competitive learning environment where outcomes seem more important than the learning process.

☐ **Make sure you are setting attainable standards and expectations.** You want to provide challenge, of course, but students build faith in their ability to succeed by experiencing success. Time invested in providing the extra scaffolding they need to meet standards and expectations will pay off.

In Summary: Self-Regulated Learning in PreK and Kindergarten

The earliest years of schooling are when students begin learning to control not only their behavior but also their emotions. They start to shift from primarily external control (Vygotsky's Stage 1) to primarily internal control (Stage 3). But even as students internalize rules and norms, the environment remains a powerful force. Lay the foundation for future academic success by providing a supportive adult relationship; modeling appropriate language and behaviors; and scaffolding students' play, conflict resolution, and pursuit of learning goals.

Self-Regulated Learning in Elementary School

Children transition from the less formal learning environment of preK and kindergarten to the more formal expectations of grades 1–5 with varying levels of self-regulation. Because we expect these students to conform to routines and complete tasks that have more steps and directions to follow and require more memory control, self-regulation can be a struggle. Some elementary students still require the kinds of support covered in the preK and kindergarten section; the others need help navigating the new challenges they face.

In the elementary school years, play remains a powerful way to develop self-regulation, although the imaginative play of early childhood should give way to more structured classroom games with set behavioral norms. Although the games should still be fun and engaging, they should be grounded in curriculum content and give students a chance to practice following directions and adhering to rules. Game playing is a way for students to cultivate resilience in the face of temporary setbacks. Losing is an inevitable part of playing games, and this helps prepare children to accept the frustration that goes along with the process of learning something difficult. The kinds of games to avoid are those that reinforce guessing as a way to answer a question and those that focus on winning, if winning is due to chance.

As children get older, motivation and social expectations begin to play a greater role in their ability to self-regulate. Social comparisons, peer influences, and parent expectations become more complex, which can make it more difficult for teachers to influence students' ability to self-regulate. From roughly upper elementary on, the teacher's role is less to help students gain control over their behaviors (although that's still relevant) and more to monitor and direct students' behavior and attention so that they can achieve goals. It requires a holistic approach that addresses both goal setting and the emotional aspects of learning, such as self-efficacy and motivation. Let's take a look.

Supporting Forethought (Grades 1–5)

Students who are self-regulated learners tend to approach long-term goals by breaking them into smaller, more achievable goals. As they achieve these smaller goals, their self-efficacy increases, and they feel more confident in their ability to take on larger challenges. Children's readiness to begin formal planning and goal-setting develops throughout the elementary years, although the exact grade varies, depending on the student. Some students may be natural planners and goal-setters while others will need more modeling and support.

What to Do: Teach Students How to Plan for Academic Success

We recommend a simple model that breaks planning into three phases: (1) setting a goal, (2) determining the strategies needed to reach the goal, and (3) deciding what resources—time and materials—are needed to reach the goal (Schunk, 2001).

Ideas to Try Now

☐ **Provide strategies to meet simple, short-term goals.** Help your students create a plan for how they will meet a simple goal (e.g., figure out where to study and at what time of day).

☐ **Teach students to track progress toward their goals.** Distribute and demonstrate how to use simple tracking tools that allow students to monitor how close they are getting to achieving each goal (e.g., checklists to be used as certain steps are completed, journals or forms for keeping track of progress).

☐ **Celebrate the achievement of short-term goals.** Acknowledge when students have attained their goal, focusing on the effort and strategies they used to do so. Reaching a goal—even an intermediate or short-term goal—can do a lot to motive students to pursue the next one.

Supporting Performance (Grades 1–5)

As students proceed through elementary school, they begin to take on more responsibility for their own learning. But what should students do when they run into a problem or assignment that they can't complete on their own? Enter *adaptive help-seeking*, in which self-regulated learners "monitor their academic performance, show awareness of difficulty they cannot overcome on their own, and exhibit the wherewithal and self-determination to remedy that difficulty by requesting assistance from a more knowledgeable individual" (Newman, 2002, p. 132).

Your less self-regulated students may not know the best ways to approach the task or which goals are most appropriate, particularly when they are encountering unfamiliar topics. Sensitivity to social comparison factors in as well. Around 1st or 2nd grade, children begin to worry about how their classmates might judge them for asking for help, which can inhibit them from using that essential self-regulated learning strategy.

What to Do: Encourage Adaptive Help Seeking

Students need to understand that it is not only OK but necessary to ask for help with work they cannot do on their own. You can support this behavior by making sure all students know

- When they need help
- That others can help
- What questions to ask to get the help they need
- That it's OK to ask for help

There are also certain grading practices and learning activities that can encourage students to seek help.

Ideas to Try Now

☐ **Post lists of "help triggers" and "help alerts."** The help trigger list provides a reminder of when students should seek help (e.g., when they don't how to get started, when they have been trying to solve a problem for more than 5 minutes, and when they are tempted to guess). The help alert list should include tips on how to indicate help is needed (e.g., raising a hand, holding up a red card) and what to say (e.g., "I am confused about ____.").

☐ **Use criterion-referenced grading.** Basing assessment on learning objectives and grading rubrics that students have seen and can understand helps create a classroom environment where content mastery is more important that "looking smart" or getting good grades. In these environments, students are more likely to ask for help when they need it. Objectives and rubrics also give students a clearer sense of where they are falling short and so they can ask more specific questions.

☐ **Use collaborative/group activities.** Group work encourages students to seek help from one another—not only because the assignments generally encourage information sharing and discussion but also because group members perceive one another as "on the same side" and find asking for help less intimidating.

Supporting Self-Reflection (Grades 1–5)

Elementary-age students remain highly sensitive to the evaluative feedback from teachers, which influences how they see themselves as learners (Harter, 1981). Now is the time to begin teaching them that they don't necessarily need another person to tell them how well they are doing; they can figure it out on their own with tools that record and track their goals, the learning strategies they use, and their learning outcomes.

What to Do: Use Portfolios

Collecting, selecting, organizing, and reflecting on a portfolio of work actively engages students in self-regulated learning. In the early elementary grades, the portfolio may include drawings, journal entries, or emergent writing pieces; in upper elementary, the portfolio should include tests or reports.

Ideas to Try Now

☐ **Provide students with a self-reflection guide.** A self-reflection guide helps students through the process of reflecting on their work with open-ended thought questions. These might include prompts such as "Why is this my best piece?", "What learning does this piece reflect?", or "This was challenging for me because of . . ." (Bower & Rolheiser, 2000). Students whose oral or written language skills may impede the reflection process can draw and label pictures.

In Summary: Self-Regulated Learning in Elementary School

By the time children complete elementary school, self-regulatory abilities are usually well established, although they may not be fully internalized until adolescence (Barkley, 1997). As students move through elementary school, they become more responsible and aware of their actions and thoughts. Over these years, teachers can do a lot to further students' self-regulation by creating a warm and supportive social climate, providing collaborative learning opportunities, and giving feedback focused on the learning process rather than the learning outcome.

If you teach elementary school, focus on supporting your students as they learn how to use self-regulatory skills like goal-setting and reflection as adaptive learning strategies. In doing so, you'll be preparing them to be effective and successful independent learners in middle and high school.

Self-Regulated Learning in Middle and High School

While the foundations of self-regulation are laid in early childhood and the elementary school years, teachers can continue to support the development and refinement of students' self-regulation into the middle and high school years. Self-regulation is associated with increased academic achievement in secondary school and beyond, and it's also a protective factor in other areas of life. For example, adolescents with higher self-regulation skills—in better control of their behavior and moods—are less susceptible to negative peer influences (Gardner, Dishion, & Connell, 2008).

As a general rule of thumb, middle and high school teachers looking to give students practice with self-regulation can do so by offering more opportunities for well-designed collaborative group work—activities that ask students to set goals and plan ahead, identify or even develop new learning strategies, carry out and reflect on the success of their plan and strategies, and modify these strategies as necessary. Adolescents, in particular, benefit from carrying out these activities within a peer group. They persist longer, demonstrate higher self-efficacy, and formulate improved problem-solving skills during a challenging task when they see their peers doing the same (Schunk & Zimmerman, 1998). Actively participating in the planning, carrying out, and discussion of and reflection on work within a group can also increase students' engagement in the classroom (Guthrie & Wigfield, 2000). As an added bonus, collaborative group work also supports students' social skills and positive social experiences with peers, which can have direct and indirect effects on their well-being and achievement (Slavin, 1995).

Now, let's look more specifically at how to support self-regulation in the secondary classroom. Because the task can be a little more complex with middle and high school students, this section includes additional information on motivation and student learning strategies.

Supporting Forethought (Grades 6–12)

As students move beyond the elementary grades and take on more academic responsibility, motivation—and the lack of it—becomes increasingly important. During the transition to middle school, self-efficacy, self-esteem, and an intrinsic interest in academic work decrease markedly, more drastically than at any other time in schooling (Wigfield et al., 1991). Understandably, self-regulated learning is affected, particularly the forethought stage, in which students think about how and why they will be completing an activity, how much effort they will invest (which is partly influenced by their interests and values), and how successful they expect to be. Every middle and high school teacher knows how challenging it can be to motivate students to engage in class and work hard toward learning goals.

An essential instructional strategy, effective even with students who claim to not be particularly interested in the content being presented, is getting them involved in goal-setting. Students who set their own goals are "more attentive to instruction, expend greater effort, and increase their confidence when they see themselves making progress" (Dembo & Eaton, 2000, p. 476). Again, planning goes hand-in-hand with goal setting, and it's important to help students set thoughtful and strategic plans to carry out their goals (Schunk, 2001).

What to Do: Help Students Set Both Long- and Short-Term Learning Goals

Long-term goals set the stage for the "bigger picture," while short-term goals provide the interim steps needed to attain the larger goal. For example, a long-term goal might be to learn new material, as reflected in performance on a unit exam. Appropriate associated short-term goals might be deciding to use (and monitor the effectiveness of) certain study strategies each week to prepare for the exam.

Ideas to Try Now

□ **Get students in the habit of setting long- and short-term goals that are both challenging and realistic.** For example, for each unit, make it common practice for students to identify the long-term goal they hope to accomplish by the end of the unit. For many students, this will likely center around getting a good grade on an exam, paper, or other project—and that's OK, but you should also encourage students to set goals that don't focus solely on their final grade. Ask students to break their long-term goal out into several short-term, manageable goals so that they can more easily monitor and track their progress toward their bigger goal. For example, students might set short-term goals related to studying: how much time they will devote to studying each week and how they will go about it. Provide strategies they can use to meet their goals. Initially, students may not be too excited about setting goals, but you'll soon see how effective goal setting can be when it comes to increasing students' motivation to learn.

What to Do: Teach Students to Use Planners and Agendas

This is strategy is an especially good one for middle school teachers, whose students are facing an increasingly heavy workload and greater expectations that they'll be able to work independently.

Ideas to Try Now

☐ **Post a weekly class agenda in your classroom and update it daily.** Create, check, and revise an ongoing agenda, evaluating your progress as you go along. Be sure to talk through your thought processes so students get a better understanding of the process.

☐ **Have students create and complete their own daily agendas.** These can be used to track assignments, projects, learning goals, and progress toward goals. You may want to check these daily agendas regularly at first to ensure that students are including relevant information (e.g., when students record an assignment, they should also include its due date and any interim steps or materials required to complete the assignment).

Supporting Performance (Grades 6–12)

During the performance phase, students put their plans into action and set out accomplish the goals they established during the forethought phase. As teachers well know, there are many factors that play into the actual "doing" of schoolwork and effect performance, among them students' motivation and confidence; the strategies they use to complete a task or learn the material; and their ability to monitor their progress, adapt their strategies, and seek help if it's needed.

It can be a challenge to motivate middle and high school students, especially when they are "bored" and expect teachers to control and alleviate their boredom. Although we all want to design learning opportunities that are interesting and engaging, we also understand that some students just aren't motivated to do the work. Self-regulated learners know how to motivate themselves even when they do not feel like performing a particular task.

Students' self-efficacy and confidence in themselves and their ability to learn something new or complete a task greatly influence their motivation (Zimmerman, 2000). When students are confident in their abilities and, importantly, view errors as an informative part of learning something new, they are significantly more likely to persist in their attempts to complete a challenging task (Dweck & Leggett, 1988). It's important that students hear messages and receive feedback from teachers, and then internalize these ideas that support their confidence and sense of self-efficacy.

What to Do: Encourage Positive Self-Talk

It may not be enough with middle and high school students to simply tell them, "you can do it" (though it certainly can't hurt), but reminding them of similar situations, activities, and problems that they have successfully navigated can be helpful, especially if they aren't making these connections themselves.

Even as adults, there are times when we're working on something new and challenging and have our doubts about whether or not we can complete the task at hand. Personal goals and interest in the task definitely play a role in your decision to keep working, but chances are you also engage in some sort of motivating self-talk.

Ideas to Try Now

☐ **Model positive self-talk in the classroom.** Though it may feel odd, it's important to model this motivational talk. For example, if you're explaining a particularly complicated math concept, you might pause at the step in the process that's likely to trip students up and say, "Now, this part looks complicated, but I'm sure that I can figure it out." You may also want to say things such as, "Let's try this and see if that works" to model that trial and error is OK and part of the learning process.

What to Do: Remember to Focus Feedback on Processes, Not Outcomes

As grade point averages, standardized test scores, and college entrance exams become increasingly important in determining students' academic futures, it can be difficult to remember that your verbal and written feedback should concentrate not on outcomes but on students' selection and use of learning processes and strategies. Doing this focuses students on what they can do to improve their work and gives them a sense of control over their academic success (Zumbrunn et al., 2011).

Ideas to Try Now

☐ **Monitor students' use of learning strategies and provide specific feedback.** It's not enough to teach students when to use various learning strategies; you must also focus their attention on the success of these strategies, teaching them to evaluate the effectiveness of their approach and revise it for next time, if necessary.

What to Do: Teach Students Both Specific and General Learning Strategies

In addition to the various content-specific learning strategies that you can and should teach students to use, don't forget to focus on three general strategies that have value across the curriculum (Dembo & Eaton, 2000):

- *Rehearsal strategies*, which involve copying material, taking verbatim notes, reciting words or definitions, underlining new material, and so on are not effective for all types of learning and, by themselves, do not lead to long-term changes in knowledge. Still, they are valuable skills to learn.

- *Elaboration strategies* are effective ways to commit newly learned information to long-term memory. They include paraphrasing, summarizing, creating analogies, and generating and answering questions.

- *Organizational strategies* are complex and effective learning strategies that require students to either find the inherent organizational structure within new material or, when a structure doesn't exist, create their own way of organizing the information. Dembo and Eaton (2000) use the organization strategy of representation or mapping in their learning strategies program for middle school students, teaching students to identify material in their textbooks and develop four possible representations for the material (e.g., hierarchies, sequences, matrices, diagrams, etc.).

Ideas to Try Now

☐ **Model the use of learning strategies.** During modeling, it's important to think aloud so that students become more aware of the cognitive processes going on "behind the scene."

☐ **Provide guided practice with learning strategies.** During guided practice, provide hints and detailed feedback to students as they execute the strategy, focusing both on what they did well and what they can do differently to improve the effectiveness of the strategy next time they use it on their own.

Once students learn different learning strategies and methods, it is important that they learn to use self-monitoring—that is, learn to track their performance and the effectiveness of the tools they use. This involves evaluating outcomes against their initial goals (e.g., did they meet their goals?), determining whether the strategy they used was effective or not, and determining their next steps (e.g., whether and how to modify the strategy if it wasn't effective or to decide to abandon that strategy and take up another). Being aware of and monitoring cognitive skills such as memory, attention, motivation, and problem solving—developing what's known as "metacognitive awareness"—is something students must do in order to become truly effective self-regulated learners (Duckworth et al., 2009).

Students can monitor their performance based on either the results of teacher-created assessments (your tests, quizzes, and assignments) or self-quizzes and other knowledge checks that they create and use themselves. Both provide formative assessment information, but the latter are a real hallmark of self-regulated learning (Cleary, Platten, & Nelson, 2008; Zumbrunn et al., 2011).

In addition to teaching students methods they can use to check their learning progress, teachers should also focus on teaching students self-recording strategies to more systematically monitor and evaluate the performance process and outcomes, including how they use their time.

What to Do: Have Students Use Learning Graphs

A picture is worth a thousand words, and monitoring and recording learning processes and behaviors in a learning graph provides students with visual representation of specific strategies, the time they spent using these strategies, and other factors ultimately related to their performance. In fact, learning graphs are key components in self-regulation interventions with adolescents (Cleary & Zimmerman, 2004). Figure 1 shows a sample learning graph. Notice that it includes multiple data points rather than data on just a single task.

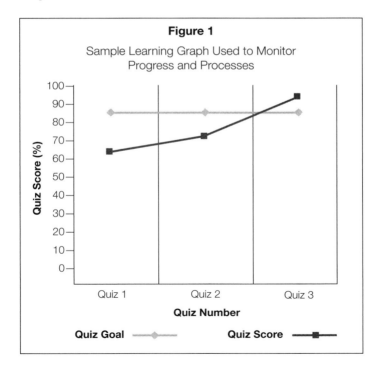

Figure 1

Sample Learning Graph Used to Monitor Progress and Processes

Given time constraints, it may not be practical to have students complete learning graphs after every single assignment or learning experience, but we recommend using them as often as possible, both after big summative assignments and throughout a unit.

Ideas to Try Now

☐ **Have students record their goal for the task and their actual performance.** Goals usually focus on learning or mastering materials and are usually measured by a grade on a task. This provides students with an opportunity to assess their actual performance against their goal.

☐ **Ask students to record the specific learning strategies and methods they used to prepare for or complete the task** (e.g., strategies used, amount of time, environmental factors). Recording this information allows students to see how different aspects relate to their performance and shows both you and them which strategies are more or less successful with any given task type. Remember to stress that failure to meet goals reflects an ineffective learning strategy, not students' innate ability.

☐ **Help students analyze their data and make strategic adjustments for future tasks.** It can be helpful to have students make specific notes about the changes they made in their learning strategies throughout a unit, a semester, or even the whole year. You could also extend learning graphs to include specific errors made on a task, which will help students find the gaps in their understanding; over time, this will allow them to identify patterns concerning which strategies are most effective for which types of tasks.

What to Do: Help Students Use Their Time Effectively

Poor time management and procrastination are common problems for middle and high school students. Learning how to use time effectively is part of becoming a self-regulated learner.

Ideas to Try Now

☐ **Have students reflect on current time-management practices.** We recommend a structured approach linked to three key questions:

1. *How do I currently use my time?* Ask students to record their activities 24 hours a day for an entire week; then have them organize their time by category and discuss differences in time usage with peers.

2. *How do I want to use my time?* Have students write academic goals for a month, plan their use of time for one week, and then evaluate the plan at the end of this period. Ask them to list and prioritize the activities they must complete to reach their goals (most important, less important, to be completed after other activities), then put the prioritized activities into students' schedules for the next week.

3. *How can I improve my control of my time?* Ask students to report on the success or failure of their new approach to time management, and get students to modify their plans as needed. (Dembo & Eaton, 2000).

☐ **Use the "bits-and-pieces approach" to make a large task manageable.** Ellis and Knaus (1977) advocate having students break work into numerous small sections and complete only a few of these sections in one sitting. For example, rather than direct students to study for an exam by rereading all three chapters the night before, encourage them to reread a few sections of each chapter every night over a two-week period.

☐ **Use the "5-minute plan."** This approach requires students to work on a task for a minimum of five minutes; at the end of five minutes, they stop and decide whether to work for another five minutes. Since getting started on a task can be the hardest part, students often choose to work in additional five-minute increments to maintain their momentum (Dembo & Eaton, 2000).

What to Do: Provide Processes to Support Homework Completion

Homework and practice contributes to academic success by providing opportunities for students to review existing skills and content and increase proficiency with new skills and content (Dean, Hubbell, Pitler, & Stone, 2012). Of course, for homework and practice to have this impact, students need to actually do it—and fostering self-regulation skills can help keep them on track.

Ideas to Try Now

☐ **Create a homework checklist or homework logs for students to use.** The log should include the time students started and completed their homework, how they motivated themselves during homework completion, how they avoided distractions, and other general behaviors.

☐ **Monitor and lead guided reflection on students' homework strategies.** Use homework logs/checklists to monitor students' approach to homework and dedicate time to reflecting on these strategies with students. Point out how the data they've captured can help them shape their future learning approaches (Ramdass & Zimmerman, 2011).

Supporting Self-Reflection (Grades 6–12)

In the final phase of self-regulated learning, students must look back on the overall performance. What worked, what didn't work, and why? How did their performance measure up against the goals they set out to accomplish? How will they apply these "lessons learned" to future learning tasks? Not surprisingly, motivation also plays an important role in this phase, as do students' self-evaluation skills. Students must also learn to manage or regulate their emotions in relation to the task outcome—not always an easy feat for a teenager!

What to Do: Teach Students to Reflect on Outcomes

Similar to how they must evaluate their learning strategies during the performance phase, students also need to learn how to reflect on their overall performance and learning. Again, it is important to model this process. At the end of each class period or larger lesson, make it common practice to reflect on the lesson and what everyone learned.

Ideas to Try Now

□ **Use question stems to help students reflect on their performance.** The following question stems can be used for both whole-class and individual student reflection:

My goal was _____ , and was/was not obtained by_____ .

I have learned_____ and/or obtained grades of_____ .

On my last assignment/project/test I did/did not reach my goal_____ .

The strategy I used was effective/ineffective because_____ .

To continue to improve, I need to change/modify_____ .

In Summary: Self-Regulated Learning in Middle and High School

The overarching goal is to help middle and high school students realize that by using effective learning strategies and study habits, they can control their learning and academic success, even when the work is challenging. According to intervention research with middle schoolers, an especially effective way to do this is to share scientific data on how learning and effort lead to physical changes in the structure of the brain. Other ways to instill a sense of control are to increase students' awareness of their strategic errors and highlight the link between strategy use and success and failure in school (Cleary & Zimmerman, 2004).

Final Thoughts

Just as all teachers know what it's like to teach students who struggle to set goals, stay on task, and stay motivated, all teachers can recognize the hallmarks of students who are able to self-regulate.

The good news is that self-regulation is not an inherent ability that students either have or don't have. It can, and should, be taught in the classroom, across grade levels, and it will help students develop the skills they need for academic success.

Yes, it takes planning and effort to incorporate the instructional strategies we have shared. Our "Ideas to Try Now" can start you down the path, but we also encourage you to examine other resources to deepen your understanding of the concept of self-regulation. We wish you the best success.

To give your feedback on this publication and
be entered into a drawing for a free ASCD
Please visit **www.ascd.org/ariasfeedback**

ENCORE

SELF-REGULATION FAQS

Q What is the difference between self-regulation and behavior management?

A While the terms are interrelated and are often used interchangeably, self-regulation and behavior management are two different things. *Self-regulation* is an internal process in which an individual uses a multifaceted set of emotional and cognitive skills (e.g., motivation, persistence, attention) to regulate his or her own behavior. Within educational literature, the term b*ehavior management* refers to external processes or rules that are imposed on students to manage their behaviors. When teachers support self-regulation skills, students learn to regulate their behavior on their own, decreasing the need for behavior management from a teacher or other adult.

Q How can I foster self-regulation with a young student who acts out physically (hitting, biting, etc.)?

A The very young need help learning how to inhibit inappropriate actions. The first step is to understand why the child acted out. After every incident, ask yourself the following questions:

- *What happened?* John took the toy Sue was playing with, which caused an argument; when Sue tried to get the toy back, John hit and kicked her.
- *What happened just prior to the behavior?* John was moving from center to center during play time.
- *How might the prior event explain the behavior?* John's frequent movement from center to center suggests that he isn't engaged in the activities provided in the centers.
- *What supports can I provide to address the prior event to ward off future occurrence of the resulting behavior?* If John has more information on the activities available in the centers, he may be more engaged and less likely to act out by taking another friend's toy or acting out physically. I might create and post activity sheets in the centers, using pictures to provide visual cues of the activities available.

Being proactive instead of reactive—in other words, providing supports to address the root cause of the physical act—not only addresses the problem now but also helps the child learn to manage his or her own behaviors so that in the future you don't have to.

Q What do I do with a 4th grader who repeatedly does not complete assignments? How about an 11th grader?

A Students don't complete their homework for reasons that are as unique as each child, which means that there isn't a single, simple strategy to address this issue. Again, the general course of action is to determine why they aren't completing their assignments:

- *Is the behavior due to a lack of motivation?* Maybe the student simply isn't interested in the topic, or maybe the work is too easy or too hard.
- *Is the behavior due to poor planning?* Perhaps the student isn't effective at setting and planning for goals or managing time.
- *Is the behavior due to a factor beyond your control?* Maybe the student has an undetected learning disability that requires additional specialized supports, or maybe there are things going on within the student's home or neighborhood that interfere with the ability to complete assignments.

Only when you get to the why of the behavior can you begin to address it.

Q How can I get families involved in fostering their child's self-regulation skills?

A Communicate. Listen. Collaborate. These strategies, which are the key to engaging families in their child's schooling (Day-Hess, 2013), are also instrumental in getting them to foster their child's self-regulation skills.

- *Communicate:* Keep families up to date about how their child is doing in the classroom—not just in terms of academic accomplishments but also in terms of self-regulation skills.
- *Listen:* Encourage families to share information or concerns about their child's behavior outside school and any thoughts they have on factors that might be affecting self-regulation.
- *Collaborate:* Work with families to ensure that children are receiving consistent support and messages at home and school to support developing self-regulation skills.

Q I'm a school principal. What kinds of policies or supports can I put in place to help teachers foster self-regulation in their students?

A Encourage schoolwide implementation of developmentally appropriate instructional practices aimed at supporting the whole child rather than just students' mastery of standards. Provide time and structures to allow for play in preK and kindergarten and cooperative learning experiences in elementary, middle, and high school. Teachers must feel free to implement strategies that further self-regulation, even though this work may not have a direct or easily measurable link to "academic" learning.

References

Anderson, P. L., & Adams, P. J. (1985). The relationship of five-year-olds' academic readiness and perceptions of competence and acceptance. *Journal of Educational Research, 79*(2), 114–118.

Barkley, R. A. (1997). Behavioral inhibition, sustained attention, and executive functions: Constructing a unifying theory of ADHD. *Psychological Bulletin, 121*, 65–94.

Blair, C. (2003). Self-regulation and school readiness. ERIC Digest. Retrieved from http://www.eric.ed.gov/ERICWebPortal/search/detailmini.jsp?_nfpb=true&_&ERICExtSearch_SearchValue_0=ED477640&ERICExtSearch_SearchType_0=no&accno=ED477640

Bodrova, E., Björk, C., Day-Hess, C., Germeroth, C., Mazzeo, D., & Isaacs, S. (2012). *Scaffolding early learning: Strategies for success.* Unpublished manuscript, Mid-continent Research for Education and Learning, Denver, CO.

Bodrova, E., & Leong, D. J. (2008). Developing self-regulation in kindergarten: Can we keep all the crickets in the basket? *Beyond the Journal: Young Children on the Web.* Retrieved from https://www.naeyc.org/files/yc/file/200803/BTJ_Primary_Interest.pdf

Bodrova, E., & Leong, D. J. (2007). *Tools of the mind* (2nd ed.). Columbus, OH: Prentice Hall.

Boekaerts, M. (2006). Self-regulation and effort investment. In K. A. Renninger & I. E. Siegel (Eds.), *Handbook of child psychology* (Vol. 4). Child psychology in practice (6th Ed., pp. 345–77). New York: John Wiley and Sons.

Bower, B., & Rolheiser, C. (2000). Portfolio assessment: Organizing for success! *Orbit, 30*(4), 47–49.

Cleary, T. J., Platten, P., & Nelson, A. (2008). Effectiveness of the self-regulation empowerment program with urban high school students. *Journal of Advanced Academics, 20*(1), 70–107.

Cleary, T. J., & Zimmerman, B. J. (2004). Self-regulation empowerment program: A school-based program to enhance self-regulated and self-motivated cycles of student learning. *Psychology in the Schools, 41*, 537–550.

Day-Hess, C. (2013, Summer). What early childhood teaches us about parent engagement. *Changing Schools, 69*, 14-15.

Dean, C. B., Hubbell, E. R., Pitler, H., & Stone, B. (2012). *Classroom instruction that works: Research-based strategies for increasing student achievement* (2nd ed.). Alexandria, VA: ASCD.

Dembo, M. H., & Eaton, M. J. (2000). Self-regulation of academic learning in middle-level schools. *The Elementary School Journal, 100*, 473–490.

Duckworth, K., Akerman, R., MacGregor, A., Salter, E., & Vorhaus, J. (2009). *Self-regulated learning: A literature review* (Research Report No. 33). Retrieved from Centre for Research on the Wider Benefits of Learning: http://www.learningbenefits.net/Publications/ResReps/ResRep33.pdf

Dweck, C. S., & Leggett, E. L. (1988). A social-cognitive approach to motivation and personality. *Psychological Review, 95*, 256–273.

Ellis, A., & Knaus, W. J. (1977). *Overcoming procrastination.* New York: New American Library.

Gardner, T. W., Dishion, T. J., & Connell, A. M. (2008). Adolescent self-regulation as resilience: Resistance to antisocial behavior within the deviant peer context. *Journal of Abnormal Child Psychology, 36*, 273–284.

Guthrie, J. T., & Wigfield, A. (2000). Engagement and motivation in reading. In M. Kamil & P. Mosenthal (Eds.), *Handbook of reading research* (Vol. 3). Mahwah, NJ: Lawrence Erlbaum Associates.

Harter, S. (1981). A new self-report scale of intrinsic versus extrinsic orientation in the classroom: Motivational and informational components. *Developmental Psychology, 17*, 300–312.

Newman, R. S. (2002). How self-regulated learners cope with academic difficulty: The role of adaptive help seeking. *Theory Into Practice, 41*(2), 132–138.

Ramdass, D., & Zimmerman, B. J. (2011). Developing self-regulation skills: The important role of homework. *Journal of Advanced Academics, 22*(2), 194–218.

Schunk, D. H. (2001). Social cognitive theory and self-regulated learning. In Zimmerman, B. J., & Schunk, D. H. (Eds.), *Self-regulated learning and academic achievement: Theoretical perspectives.* Mahwah, NJ: Lawrence Erlbaum Associates.

Schunk, D. H., & Ertmer, P. (2000). Self-regulation and academic learning: Self-efficacy enhancing interventions. In J. Boekaerts, P. Pintrich, & M. Zeidner (Eds.), *Handbook of self-regulation.* Burlington, MA: Elsevier Academic Press.

Schunk, D. H., & Zimmerman, B. J. (1998). *Self-regulated learning: From teaching to self-reflective practice*. New York: Guilford.

Shonkoff, J. P., & Phillips, D. A. (Eds.). (2000). *From Neurons to neighborhoods: The science of early childhood development*. Washington, DC: National Academies Press.

Slavin, R. E. (1995). *Cooperative learning* (2nd ed.). Boston: Allyn and Bacon.

Vygotsky, L. S. (1997). *Educational psychology* (R. Silverman, Trans.). Boca Raton, FL: St. Lucie Press.

Wigfield, A., Eccles, J., MacIver, D., Reuman, D., & Midgley, C. (1991). Transitions during early adolescence: Changes in children's domain specific self-perceptions and general self-esteem across the transition to junior high school. *Developmental Psychology, 27*, 552–565.

Wilson, K. M., & Trainin, G. (2007). First-grade students' motivation and achievement for reading, writing, and spelling. *Reading Psychology, 28*(3), 257–282.

Zimmerman, B. J. (2000). Attainment of self-regulation: A social cognitive perspective. In M. Boekaerts, P. Pintrich, & M. Zeidner (Eds.), *Handbook of self-regulation, research, and applications* (pp. 13–39). Orlando, FL: Academic Press.

Zimmerman, B. J. (2008). Investigating self-regulation and motivation: Historical background, methodological developments, and future prospects. *American Educational Research Journal, 45*, 166–183.

Zumbrunn, S., Tadlock, J., & Roberts, E. D. (2011). *Encouraging self-regulated learning in the classroom: A review of the literature*. Unpublished manuscript, Metropolitan Educational Research Consortium, Virginia Commonwealth University, Richmond, VA. Retrieved from http://merc.soe.vcu.edu/Reports/Self%20Regulated%20Learning.pdf

Related Resources

At the time of publication, the following ASCD resources were available (ASCD stock numbers appear in parentheses). For up-to-date information about ASCD resources, go to www.ascd.org. You can search the complete archives of Educational Leadership at http://www.ascd.org/el.

ASCD EDge®

Exchange ideas and connect with other educators interested in self-regulated learning on the social networking site ASCD EDge at http://ascdedge.ascd.org/

Print Products

The Best Schools: How Human Development Research Should Inform Educational Practice by Thomas Armstrong (#106044)

Causes & Cures in the Classroom: Getting to the Root of Academic and Behavior Problems by Margaret Searle (#113019)

Developing Minds: A Resource Book for Teaching Thinking (3rd ed.) edited by Arthur L. Costa (#101063)

Getting to "Got It!": Helping Struggling Students Learn How to Learn by Betty K. Garner (#107024)

ASCD PD Online® Courses

The Brain: Developing Lifelong Learning Habits (2nd ed.) (#PD11OC136)

For more information: send e-mail to member@ascd.org; call 1-800-933-2723 or 703-578-9600, press 2; send a fax to 703-575-5400; or write to Information Services, ASCD, 1703 N. Beauregard St., Alexandria, VA 22311-1714 USA.

About the Authors

Carrie Germeroth, Ph.D, a former early childhood consultant at Mid-continent Research for Education and Learning (McREL), is assistant director of research at the Marsico Institute for Early Learning and Literacy at the University of Denver (DU), where she conducts research and publishes widely in the areas of social emotional development and early childhood classroom quality. A member of the Colorado Department of Education's School Readiness assessment subcommittee, she also served as project manager on the development of Colorado's Early Learning and Development Guidelines as well as the Pre-Kindergarten Standards for the State of North Dakota.

Crystal Day-Hess, Ph.D, is a senior researcher and lead of the Early Childhood team at McREL, where she develops and delivers professional development training and conducts research. She has extensive experience developing, coordinating, and conducting literature reviews and empirical research in the early childhood field. Prior to joining McREL, she was a research assistant and instructor at the University of Louisville. Her work in the Early Intervention for Families Lab in the Department of Psychological and Brain Sciences broadly focused on young children's cognitive, social, and emotional school readiness skills.

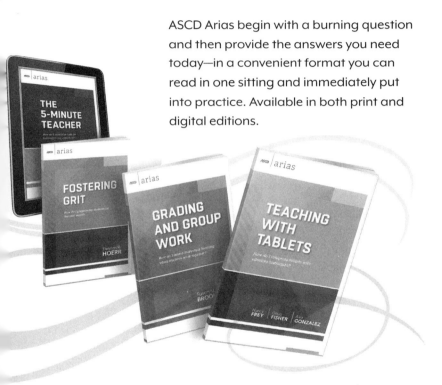